Latinas of the FUTURE
Advice from the heart

The Fig Factor Foundation

Latinas of the Future

© Copyright 2022, The Fig Factor Foundation
All rights reserved.

No portion of this book may be reproduced by mechanical, photographic or electronic process, nor may it be stored in a retrieval system, transmitted in any form or otherwise be copied for public use or private use without written permission of the Copyright Owner.

It is sold with the understanding that the publisher and the individual authors are not engaged in the rendering of psychological, legal, accounting or other professional advice. The content and views in each chapter are the sole expression and opinion of its author and not necessarily the views of Fig Factor Media, LLC.

For more information, contact:
Fig Factor Media, LLC | www.figfactormedia.com
The Fig Factor Foundation | www.thefigfactor.org

Cover Design & Layout by Juan Pablo Ruiz
Printed in the United States of America

ISBN: 978-1-957058-34-4
Library of Congress Control Number: 2022936856

DEDICATION

To all of the young Latinas
with big dreams.

TABLE OF CONTENTS

Introduction..5

Advice from **Blanca Sepulveda**..
Advice from **Claudia Martinez**..
Advice from **Elizabeth Villarreal**..
Advice from **Jacqueline S. Ruiz**..
Advice from **Judith Banda-Guzmán**..
Advice from **Leonor Gil**..
Advice from **Maria Herrera Paloma**..
Advice from **Priscilla Guasso**..
Advice from **Ximena Atristain-Bigurra**..

INTRO

As Latinas, we live in a world where we are ready to achieve the greatest but are often faced with obstacles, whether they come from family or anywhere else. Though those obstacles might delay our paths to success, they shouldn't stop us. We must teach ourselves and those who come after us that being a Latina is something to be proud about and that anything is achievable regardless of gender or culture.

We must start with you, our Young Latinas. The future that you have painted for yourself is only a mile away but in order to get there, you must be willing take that first step. The advice given in this book is meant to motivate, inspire, and move you to make those dreams into realities. As we have paved a path for you, you must continue to strengthen that path for our future generations.
This advice is from some of the most successful Latinas, but they didn't start this way. They have faced numerous challenges but despite them, they have risen to the top of their careers. You can do it too!

Happy Young Latina Day, April 11.
May you all continue to dream big and achieve bigger!

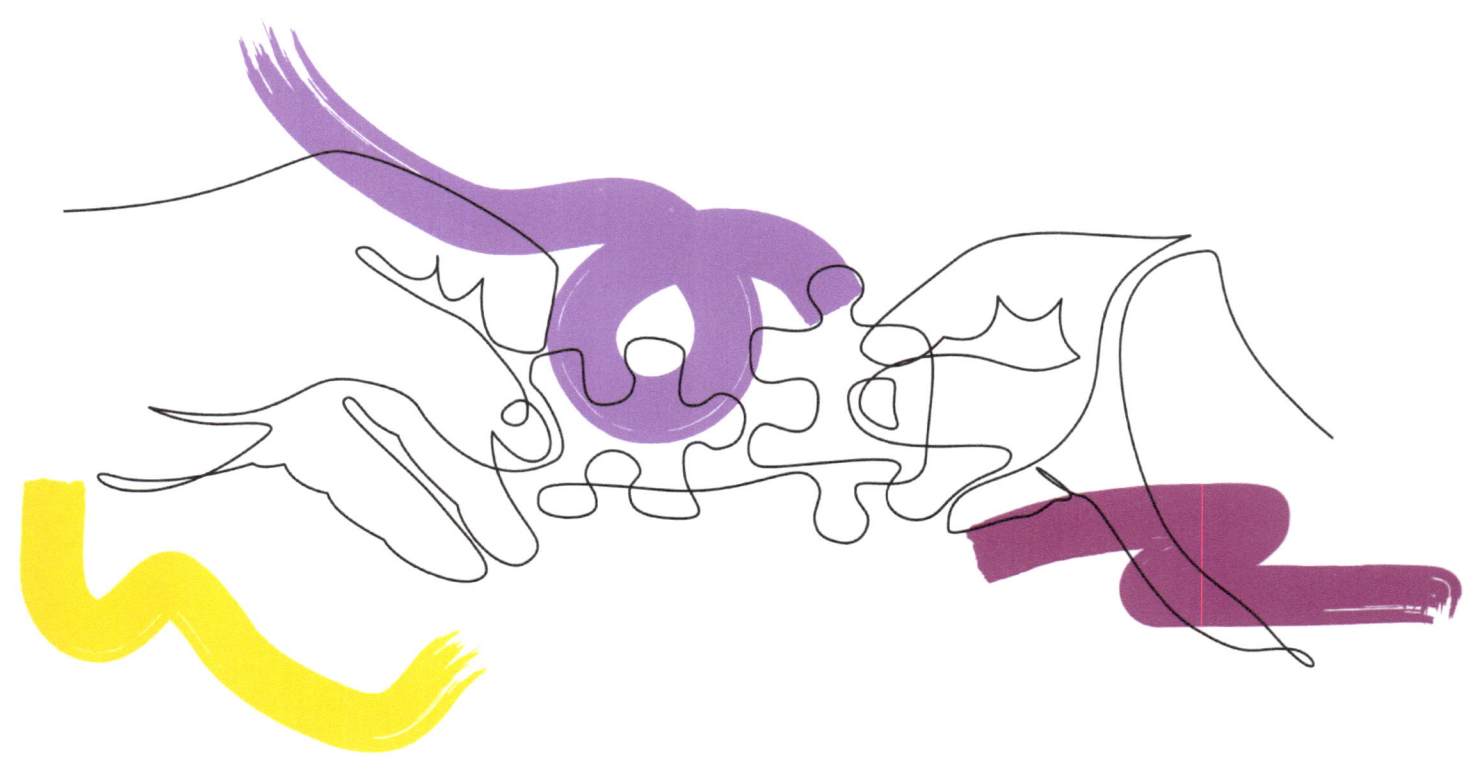

Advice from **Blanca Sepulveda**

Seek mentorship in the areas you'd like to improve on or pursue. Mentors can share valuable information based on their experiences and knowledge and help build your network. You can share your doubts and fears and they will guide you and coach you. Be open to feedback and be courageous and vulnerable to get the most help and encouragement you need. **Always understand that setbacks are part of growth and gaining experiences.**

Don't be afraid to trust your mentors and take risks to reach different growth levels. Remember to have fun along the way. The journey of growth takes time so have some patience and always stay positive.

ABOUT BLANCA:

Blanca has over 20 years of banking experience. She took a bold leap of faith and opened her own business, Transformation Financial. She mentors, trains and develops others to become entrepreneurs in the finance industry. Blanca and her team help families from all walks of life create a better financial future. She partners up with many community-based organizations to bring financial awareness to help families and individuals through free workshops and consultations. Blanca is a proud mom of her son Christian, loves spending time with family and enjoys traveling.

Advice from **Claudia Martinez**

Your circumstances today do not define where you will end up. Make sure you get the help you need to be able to succeed. Through therapy, mentorship, and personal development I have been able to get to where I am today.

Everything in life is happening as it should. Even if you are struggling at the moment, ask yourself what can I learn from this. Trust Life. Trust the process. But especially, always trust yourself. Be your biggest advocate, cheerleader, and love yourself. Believe in yourself. If you adapt your thinking to this it will allow you to grow from every hardship you experience. I believe in YOU! Keep going!

ABOUT CLAUDIA:

Claudia Martinez was born and raised in Acambaro, Guanajuato. Claudia moved to the United States at the age of 8 where she learned English shortly after. With a lot of grit and determination, she was the first in her family to graduate from a four-year University. Claudia is Co-Author of Today's Inspired Young Latina Volume II and board member of the Fig Factor Foundation where she also serves as a mentor. She has also been featured in panels at Univision and UCLA. She is an expert in influencer marketing and has worked with brands such as VW Taos and T-Mobile. Her current role is Manager of Creator Campaigns and Partnerships.

Advice from **Elizabeth Villarreal**

Don't be afraid to fail, because if you don't fail you will never grow.

Failures are lessons we go thru in life, in order to become a strong confident woman.

Fail and Fail again until you succeed. **Don't give up on you!**

ABOUT ELIZABET:

Elizabeth Villarreal has been a Client Solution Executive with AT&T for twenty years. She received her Bachelors in Marketing. She is an author, entrepreneur, and a proud single mom of a young man at DePaul University. She serves on the board as the Vice President for the Fig Factor Foundation. A Foundation, working with young Latinas. She is passionate about mentoring and inspiring Latina leaders as well as working with women to dream again. She believes dreams and goals are attainable which starts with the Belief in ourselves. That is the message she wants to spread to other women.

Advice from **Jacqueline S. Ruiz**

Believe in yourself. Believe that there is something greater to achieve. Believe that there are good people in the world that guide you on your journey. Believe that the world is filled with extraordinary opportunities. Believe that you can change the world with the beautiful energy that emanates from your heart.

Believe that value of knowledge and willingness to serve others can be translated into real abundance. Believe that dreams are for you to achieve them. Believe that you can achieve anything you set your mind to. Believe that we believe in you.

You are our future.

ABOUT JACQUELINE:

Jacqueline Camacho-Ruiz is the CEO of JJR Marketing and Fig Factor Media LLC international book publishing company, founder of The Fig Factor Foundation, creator of Today's Inspired Latina book series and international movemen, author of 30 books, international speaker, and pilot. Jacqueline speaks to hundreds of audiences about marketing, servant leadership, finding your passion, and achieving success in business. She has addressed the United States Army, Airbus, BP International, United Airlines, Allstate, Northern Trust US + Europe and Farmers Insurance among other corporations to share her inspiration. She has been featured in Forbes, INC Magazine, Univision, Telemundo, ABC 7, WTTW, NBC 5, among others.

Advice from **Judith Banda-Guzmán**

Work on yourself every day, always looking to **turn yourself into a better version of you.** Look to heal your inner self. Changes don't happen overnight. When you turn into the person that you want to BE, the people that are meant to be in your life will begin to appear and will help you achieve your dreams.

In order to accomplish this, start with little things like reading a book, listening to a podcase, attending a class/course or self-help workshops. Surround yourself with people that positively impact you and seek help if you need to but never quit growing in all aspects of your life. Always look for the next level up in every one of them.

ABOUT JUDITH:

Judith Banda-Guzman is a Research Professor in the division of Engineering at the Department of Art and Business in Campus Irapuato-Salamanca. She received a Doctorate in Accounting and Finance from the University of Trujillo and has participated as a speaker at international conferences. Judith won recognition by the Small Business Institute for the best conceptual paper entitled "Personal Characteristics of Successful Women entrepreneurs in Mexico." She is also co-author of Today's Inspired Latinas Volume IV, coordinator of the book Jóvenes Soñadoras, and co-author of the book "LovethruCovid19"

Advice from **Leonor Gil**

As a young Latina woman, you are faced with a myriad of responsibilities, demands, pressures, choices and decisions to make. Growing up you may have lacked the resources, the mentors and the type of advice to help you overcome these challenges.

Remember that we are all made in God's image. You must believe that you have ALL you need inside of you, in your heart and in your mind and soul to accomplish any goal you set for yourself. It is your mindset that is so powerful and controls your every move. **Anything you think you are; you shall become.** You are formidable beyond measure. You have overcome so many things in your life already. You have outgrown past versions of yourself. You have come a long way, but it is more exciting to know how much farther you will go.

ABOUT LEONOR:

Leonor Gil is a professional in the financial services industry with a depth of experience providing financial education. Leonor's purpose in life is to help others. Leonor received the Chairman's Award – D&I in 2017 and the Mujeres de HACE Leadership Award in 2018. Leonor enjoys positively impacting the lives of others by volunteering in various capacities such as for Big Brothers, Big Sister for United Way, and as a Confirmation Facilitator at her church. She serves as a mentor to co-workers, and to young Latinas for The Fig Factor Foundation, where she also serves as a board member and officer. Leonor is a published contributing author to Today's Inspired Latina Volume V. Leonor is a proud mother or two children, Jorge and Carol, and a proud grandmother to four grandchildren; Destiny, Anthony, Santino and Jaylani! Her hobbies include hiking, dancing, and spending time with the family.

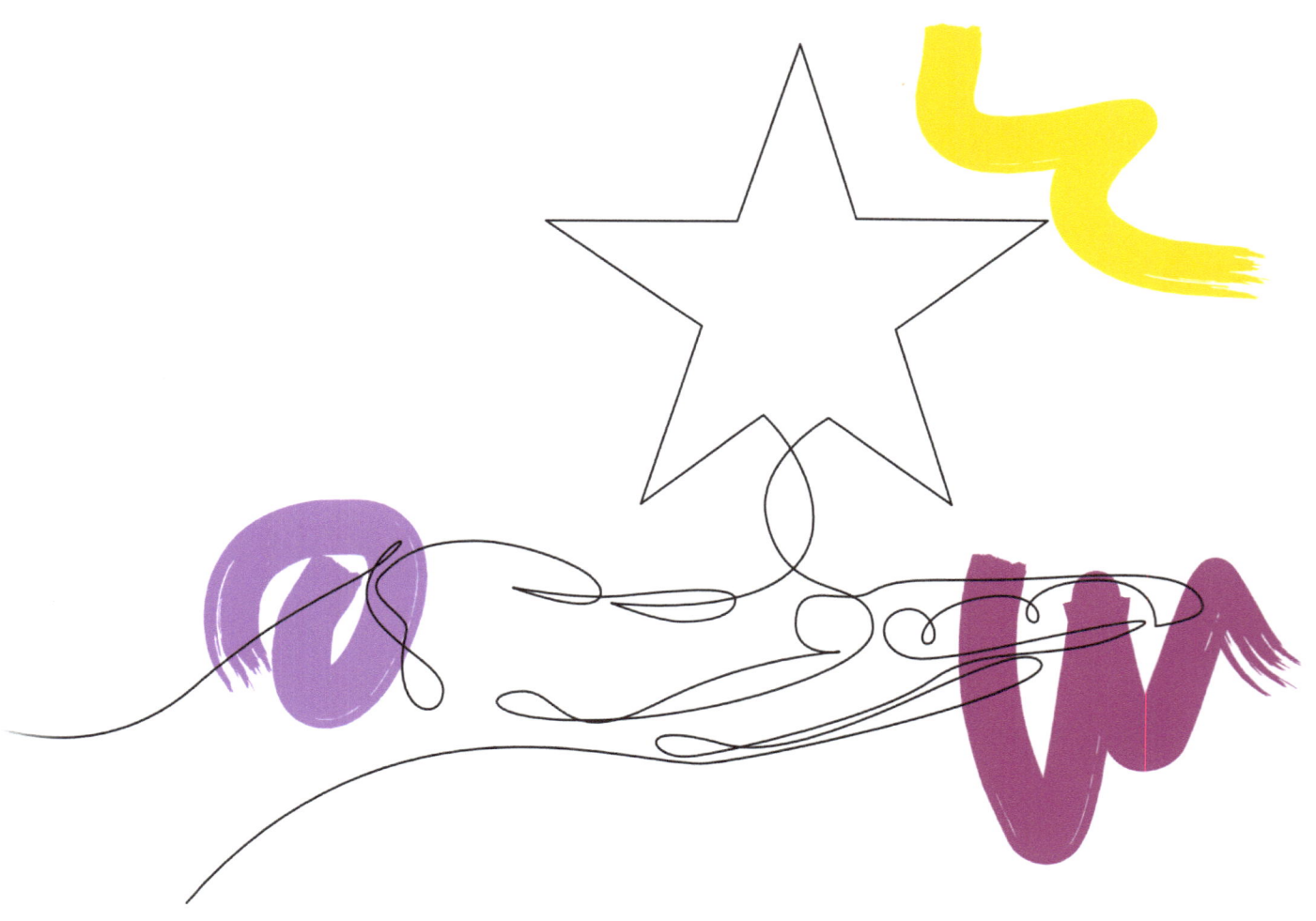

Advice from **Maria Herrera Paloma**

If you are anything like I was as a Young Latina growing up in a traditional Latino household, then you have big dreams, are hard-working and have big Faith and goals. Yet, you are surrounded by doubt and fear and maybe even people who don't quite understand or support you.

You have all the answers right inside of your very self. Face your fears and challenges, allow these to help you grow as you consistently learn and seek knowledge so that you may continue to grow. We are constantly a work in progress and you must strive to progress each and every day!

ABOUT MARIA:

Maria considers herself an agent of change. She sees how Latinas are reaching new heights in business, government and the courts and believes there is more progress to be made. This is the revolutionary part of how she was raised and what she hopes to instill in young Latinas as our current President of The Fig Factor Foundation, as a Dual Language Educator, and a coach within the WISE community. She is also a RYT-200 Yoga Instructor teaching within her community. As a Financial Coach entrepreneur, she is building a terrific Holistic Wellness following that focuses not only on the physical and mental wellness but also the financial realm. She is Mexican-born and the youngest of 9 siblings and is happily married to Miguel Ricardo, her husband of over 30 years. She has three wonderful adult children: Sofia, Miguel and Sam.

Advice from **Priscilla Guasso**

Do not burn bridges. **Be the one that helps find a middle ground, even in the worst of situations.** Sometimes that may mean you need to end certain relationships and that is ok. Over time you'll learn that all things that end do not have to end dramatically or negatively, they can just be that —an end.

Take the higher road and don't get involved in the drama because there is enough negativity in this world. Focus your energy on spaces that bring more positivity and light around you. It'll change your world in ways you'll have never dreamed of.

ABOUT PRISCILLA:

Based in Miami and Chicago, Priscilla Guasso thrives in leading human resources teams focused on all areas of the employee life cycle. Her sixteen years of global experience expands to HR in the US, Latin America, Caribbean, UK and Canada within the hospitality, healthcare and as a current leader of Talent Management in the technology industry. Through her business Manifesting Leadership Group, LLC she thoroughly enjoys coaching and training leaders to invest in themselves to effectively grow their leadership skills in corporate, startups, nonprofit and government. As an Amazon Best Selling Author and founder of *Latinas Rising Up In HR®* she continues to give back by creating a community of Latinas in HR (and allies) sharing their keys of knowledge and success to O-P-E-N doors of unlimited possibilities!

Advice from **Ximena Atristain-Bigurra**

Remember that when you fall, you can always get up and learn from those obstacles. **Focus on having a good self-worth and having a passion that drives you;** build your character as you do what you love and never stop believing in yourself.

That's what Fig Factor is, we are all here to support you and believe in you as young powerful women.

ABOUT XIMENA:

Ximena M. Atristain-Bigurra is a professional in the beauty industry. A native of Bolivia, is a leader, an entrepreneur, an avid performing arts lover, and off course, a beauty industry connoisseur. Ximena earned her Bachelor's degree from Columbia College in Interior Design and an Associate degree in Fashion Design from Harper College. Upon graduation, she worked in an architectural firm and then started her business called Designs by Ximena, a fashion and dressmaking business. Later, she moved into the beauty industry and has been working in this industry for over 20 years. She represents the Orlane brand at Neiman Marcus in Oakbrook, Il. In her 20 years in the beauty industry, she has been doing facials, promoting very upscale skin care products, make-up for weddings, quinceañeras, special occasions, run-shows, and more. Ximena reopened her Business Designs by Ximena when the pandemic came along and started sewing face masks in different styles, lately she has been designing Bridal Veils, Clothes, specialty bags and more.